The Truck Driver's Cookbook

BY JIM WYNN

THE

TRUCK DRIVERS

COOKBOOK

Re-order
Additional copies
From

Jim Wynn Farms
P.O. Box 730
Lumber City, Ga. 31549

The Truck Drivers Cookbook comes packaged in a most unique burlap bag.

This cookbook is a perfect gift for birthdays, holidays, weddings, anniversaries or just a great gift for any day.

Jim Wynn
P.O. Box 730
Lumber City, Ga. 31549
e-mail: jswynn@altamaha.net
Phone: (912) 363-8401

Thanks
We hope you enjoy

Jim Wynn & Toni Buford

Published by Jim Wynn
Complete book design by Jim Wynn & Toni Buford

ISBN 0-9705528-0-7

Jim Wynn
P.O. Box 730
Lumber City, Ga. 31549

Printed in the USA by

WIMMER
The Wimmer Companies
Memphis
1-800-548-2537

Introduction
By: Jim Wynn

In 1946, my grandfather Ray Wynn Sr. (Pop) started hauling watermelons and pears to the Atlanta Farmers Market in a 2 ton open truck. In 1954 or 1955, he took me with him. In a few years I was selling watermelons 3 for $1.00 and having a big time. I lived on a farm most of my young years; always having plenty of fresh fruit, vegetables and meat in season.

My goodness how things have changed. Today our restaurants and grocery stores have fresh fruit, vegetables, meats and seafood almost 365 days a year. Thanks to the truckers; while most of us are sleeping, truck drivers are hauling freight and thinking about a good place to eat and rest when they have time to stop.

Many restaurants are open 24 hours a day. Some of the hardest working people in America are waitresses, waiters, cooks and chefs; waiting to serve us.

Thank goodness for the American truckers, we have access to the best of everything the world has to offer.

ACKNOWLEDGEMENTS

I would like to thank our truck drivers and their families; and all friends who have helped make this book possible.

Cynthia Wynn Shuman, Cindy & Brad Burgess, Lee Buford, Kitty Darby, Mavis Herndon, Linda Smith, Brian & Rose Engstrom, Janice Ray, Nancy Pihlstrom, Frank T. Kolb, Wayne Romamn, Ava Beecher, Susan Webster, Freddie Strange, Wayne & Rosalind Powell, Doris & Roy Meyers, Paul Geda, Carolyn Thompson, Gail & Bill Jordan, Charlene Buford and Connie Morgan.

And a special thanks to Toni Buford, I couldn't have done it without you. And many, many thanks to all of you.

TABLE OF CONTENTS

SNACKS

Zell's parmesan tomatoes (Goes with everything)
Slice good ripe tomatoes, salt and pepper and sprinkle with
Parmesan cheese. Stick under broiler until heated. Compliments
any meal.

Fried Sweet Potatoes. Peel sweet potatoes and slice into thin slices.
Fry in oil until done. Put on platter and sprinkle with powdered
sugar. Great with any meal or snack.

Fig preserves and hot biscuits. Slice biscuits in half and spread
butter on both sides and add fig preserves. Simply delicious.

Fresh fruit. Please eat some every day.

MY FAVORITE SANDWICHES AS A KID AND ADULT

Tomato sandwich. Slice 2 or 3 slices of vine ripe tomato on your favorite bread. Spread some mayonnaise on both sides of bread. Salt and pepper to taste. WOW

Banana sandwich. Slice bananas in thin slices and spread over sandwich bread, add mayonnaise and ENJOY.

Pineapple sandwich. Sliced or crushed pineapple on sandwich bread with mayonnaise, GREAT.

Pork chop sandwich. Fried pork chop with a slice of onion, ketchup and mayonnaise on sandwich bread or biscuit.

Irish potato sandwich. Slice potatoes in thin slices and fry in oil until done. Put mayonnaise on both slices of sandwich bread and add potatoes, TRY IT.

Biscuit and Syrup.
My all time favorite as a kid. When I would get home from school; there was always leftover biscuits covered on the stove. I would take a biscuit and stick my finger ¾ way down in the biscuit and pour syrup in it.
Stop laughing now, this is true and it was very good.

Recipe Notes

APPETIZERS,
BRUNCH
AND BREAD

SHRIMP BALLS

1   *medium onion, chopped*
1   *medium raw potato, diced*
1 ½   *pounds of raw shrimp*
1   *egg*
       salt and pepper to taste
       oil for frying

*Chop onions, potato, and shrimp. Stir in egg, salt and pepper.
Batter must be thick. Drop by teaspoon into hot oil and fry
until brown.*

SHRIMP SPREAD

1	8oz. package cream cheese
½	cup mayonnaise
1	4 ½ oz. can tiny shrimp, drained
½	cup finely chopped celery
½	cup finely chopped onions
1 ½	teaspoons lemon juice
1 ½	teaspoons Worcestershire sauce

Combine softened cream cheese and mayonnaise; beat until smooth. Blend in remaining ingredients. Mix well, chill and serve with crackers. Best when refrigerated overnight.

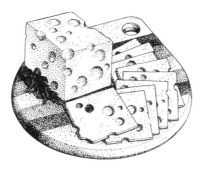

SALMON SPREAD

1	can salmon
1	8 oz. package cream cheese
1	Tablespoon lemon juice
2	teaspoons onion, diced
1	teaspoon horseradish (I like creamy)
¼	teaspoon liquid smoke
1	teaspoon minced parsley

Mix ingredients and chill.

CHUCK'S ONION DIP

1	*jumbo onion, chopped*
2	*Tablespoons sliced black olives*
3	*Tablespoons olive oil*
1 ½	*teaspoons wine vinegar*
	dash of Worcestershire sauce
3	*Tablespoons chopped green chili peppers*
1	*large tomato, peeled and chopped*
	dash of tabasco sauce
	salt and pepper to taste

Combine the above ingredients and chill well. Serve with chips.

MOM'S QUICHE

1	pie crust, unbaked, pricked
¾	cup onion, diced
½	cup ham, diced
3	Tablespoons margarine
1 ½	cups of mild American cheese, grated
1	cup Swiss cheese, grated
1	cup of caraway seed cheese, grated
¼	cup evaporated milk
2	eggs
½	cup sour cream
½	cup crumbled bacon

Melt margarine in skillet and saute onions and ham until done. Place in bottom of unbaked pie crust. Mix cheese, milk, eggs and sour cream; and pour atop onion and ham mixture. Bake at 350 degrees for 30 minutes and garnish with crumbled bacon. Can be served for a brunch with fresh fruit.

HAM AND BROCCOLI QUICHE

2   frozen pie crusts
1   cup cooked chopped ham
2   eggs, beaten
¾   cup grated cheddar cheese
¾   cup grated or thin slices Swiss cheese
1   10oz. package of frozen chopped Broccoli
1   onion, chopped
1   small can or jar chopped mushrooms, drained
1/3   cup milk
        salt and pepper

Cook broccoli according to directions, drain and pour in bowl. Add 2 beaten eggs, all of the cheeses, mushrooms, onions, milk, salt, pepper and chopped ham. Pour into both pie crusts. Bake at 375 degrees for about 50 minutes.

CHARLIE'S EGG OMELET

2   *eggs, beaten*
1   *small onion, chopped*
1   *medium bell pepper, chopped*
2   *slices ham, chopped*
2   *Tablespoons cooking oil*
      Salt to taste
1   *slice cheddar cheese, chopped*

Put oil in skillet; and let it get hot. In a bowl add eggs, onion, bell pepper, ham and salt to taste. Beat slightly. Cook on medium heat and when oil gets hot add egg mixture. Watch closely and turn. When you turn the first time you can add the cheese and let it melt.

SPANISH EGG SALAD SANDWICH

½   cup sour cream
3   Tablespoons canned chopped green chilies, drained
1   Tablespoon lemon juice
1   teaspoon salt
2   teaspoons taco sauce
9   hard boiled eggs, chopped
6   slices tomato
6   slices whole wheat bread, toasted
1   cup shredded Monterey Jack cheese

Combine first 5 ingredients in a medium bowl; stir well. Gently stir in chopped eggs. Place 1 tomato slice on each slice of toasted bread. Spread about ½ cup egg mixture over each tomato slice. Sprinkle evenly with cheese. Place on an ungreased baking sheet. Broil 5 ½ inches from heat (with electric oven door partially opened) 3 minutes or until cheese melts. Serve sandwiches immediately.

MEXICAN CORNBREAD

1	cup self-rising cornmeal
2	eggs
1	cup American cheese, grated
1	4 oz. can red chili peppers, chopped
½	teaspoon salt
½	teaspoon pepper
1	7 oz. can cream style corn
¾	cup milk
1/3	cup salad oil

Mix cornmeal, salt and pepper. Mix in eggs, corn, cheese and milk. Mix red peppers and oil; pour into corn mixture. Mix well; pour into well-greased iron frying pan. Bake at 400 degrees for 40 minutes.

VEGETABLES
AND
SIDES

CALICO BEANS

1	pound of hot bulk sausage(fried and drained)
1	large can of Bush's baked beans
2	cans of lima beans
2	cans of butter beans
1	can of kidney beans
½	small bottle of bar-b-que sauce

(optional) onion and green pepper if desired

Combine all ingredients and simmer on low heat for approximately 1 hour.

THREE BEAN SALAD

1	can waxed beans
1	can green beans
1	can kidney beans
1	small onion, chopped
½	cup green pepper, chopped

Combine ingredients and mix well.

Dressing:

2	cups apple cider vinegar
	enough honey to sweeten to your taste

Refrigerate for a day or two before eating.

GREEN BEAN CASSEROLE

1	medium onion, chopped
2	Tablespoons butter
3	15 ½oz. cans of cut green beans
	bacon drippings
1	8oz. can water chestnuts, drained
1 ½	cups grated cheddar cheese
2	15 oz. cans cream of mushroom soup
	Ritz cracker crumbs

Chop onion. Saute in butter until tender. Cook green beans with a small amount of bacon drippings until most of the liquid has evaporated. Slice water chestnuts and add to beans. Mix onions, cheese and mushroom soup with beans. Pour into casserole dish. Sprinkle with Ritz crackers; bake at 350 degree until bubbly.

CABBAGE SALAD

½	medium head of cabbage, chopped
2	cups of chopped tomatoes
1	cup of chopped green peppers
1	cup of sliced green onions, including tops
1	cup cubed mild cheddar cheese
¼	cup of grated carrots
¾	cup mayonnaise
1/3	cup milk
¼	teaspoon salt (optional)

In a large bowl, combine cabbage, tomatoes, green pepper, green onions, cheddar cheese and carrots; mix well. In a small bowl, combine mayonnaise, milk and salt; whisk until smooth. Pour over vegetables and toss gently. Chill overnight.

JACK'S FAMOUS COLE SLAW

1	*small red cabbage, chopped fine*
1	*small green cabbage, chopped fine*
1	*medium yellow onion, chopped fine*
1	*medium red onion, chopped fine*
2	*cups of cherry tomatoes, cut in half*
	lightly salt and pepper to taste
3	*Tablespoons of real mayonnaise*

Stir well.
If that's not enough mayonnaise to suit you add more. Add an 8oz. can of crushed pineapple.(Stir, stir, stir well and chill)then serve.

Yield: 6 to 8 servings

BAILEY'S COLESLAW

1   *small head of cabbage cored, sliced thin long strands*
1   *bunch green onions chopped fine*
1   *cup of real mayonnaise*
¼   *cup apple cider vinegar*
¼   *cup sugar*
1   *teaspoon salt*
1   *Tablespoon pepper*
1   *Tablespoon garlic powder*

Mix all ingredients well in a bowl and let sit for 6 hours before serving. Best if made the day before.

Serves: 6 to 10

MAMMY'S CORNBREAD, BROCCOLI SOUFFLE

1	*6oz. package of cornbread mix(follow directions on box for mixture)*
1	*10oz. package of frozen broccoli, chopped and drained*
1	*stick of butter, chopped in slices*
1	*cup Swiss cheese*
3	*eggs, well beaten*
1	*small onion, chopped*

Mix all ingredients well, pour in a baking pan or skillet and bake at 350 degrees for 25 to 30 minutes. ENJOY.

CARROT SALAD

1   lb. carrots
1   cup raisins
1   can pineapple or mandarin orange
1   cup apple cider vinegar
¾   cup honey

Grate up carrots and mix with raisins and fruit. Stir up vinegar and honey until honey dissolves. Pour over carrot mixture. Keep cool.

EMMA'S SUE'S COLLARD GREENS

1   large bunch of collard greens

Take bunch of collard greens and strip leaves from stem and cut leaves in small pieces and wash very good. In a large cooking pot add 3 quarts of water and add greens and boil about 15 minutes. Add 2 smoked neck bones and several slices of bacon. Boil for 30 to 45 minutes and add hot water if needed. Salt and pepper to taste. Extra good with hot sauce.

MISS LEE'S GREENS

1   **bunch of collards**
1   **bunch of mustards**
       salt to taste
1   **Tablespoon of fried meats grease**

Clean mustards and collards very good. Cut up collards and put in a large cooking pot and add enough water so the collards will be covered. Add salt and bring to a boil and cook for 20 minutes. While collards are cooking; cut up mustards. Then add mustards to collards and add fried meats grease and cook until tender.

CORN, PEPPER AND ONION CASSEROLE

1   *can cream style corn*
½   *cup green peppers, chopped*
¾   *cup onions, diced*
2   *Tablespoons margarine*
3   *Tablespoons pimento, diced and drained*
4   *eggs, slightly beaten*

Saute green peppers and onions in margarine. Add corn, pimento and eggs. Pour in greased pan and bake at 350 degrees for 25 minutes or until firm. (Optional: may top with French fried onion rings or cracker crumbs).

JIM'S BAKED ONIONS

Peel a large onion and core out center of onion ¾ way down. Salt and pepper lightly. Pack 1/3 butter, 1/3 bacon bits, and 1/3 Monterey Jack cheese. On outside of onion wrap with 2 strips of bacon and secure with toothpick. Wrap onion in tin foil being careful not to puncture foil. Pre-heat oven to 350 degrees and bake approximately 40-45 minutes. Check occasionally as you would for baked potato for desired softness.

SOUTHERN ONION PIE

1	cup of Ritz cracker crumbs
½	stick of butter, melted
2	cups of onion, thinly sliced
3	Tablespoons butter
2	eggs
¾	cup milk
¾	teaspoon salt
	dash of pepper
¼	cup grated sharp cheddar cheese
	paprika
	parsley

Mix Ritz cracker crumbs and melted butter. Press into 8-inch pie plate. Saute onions with 2 tablespoons of butter until clear, not brown. Spoon into pie crust. Beat eggs with milk, salt, pepper and pour over onions. Sprinkle with cheese and paprika. Bake at 350 degrees for 30 minutes or until center is firm. Sprinkle with parsley before serving.

SWEET ONION GRITS

8	slices of bacon
1	16 oz, can tomatoes, undrained and chopped
1	medium onion, chopped
2	small green peppers, finely chopped
¼	teaspoon sugar
6	cups of water
1	teaspoon salt
1 ½	cups uncooked regular grits

Cook bacon slices in skillet until crisp. Drain bacon; crumble and set aside. Pour off drippings, reserving two tablespoons in skillet. Saute onion and green pepper in drippings; stir in tomatoes and sugar. Bring to a boil; reduce heat and simmer 30 minutes, stirring occasionally. Bring water and salt to a boil; add grits. Cook 10-20 minutes, stirring frequently, until grits are thickened. Remove from heat; stir in tomato mixture. Spoon into serving dish; sprinkle bacon on top.

Yield: 8 servings.

CINDY'S FRIED ONION RINGS

5	large onions
1 ¼	cup all purpose flour
	dash salt
1	slightly beaten egg
1 ¼	cups milk
1	teaspoon vegetable oil

Combine ingredients and beat until you have a good moist batter. Slice onions about ¼-inch thick. Separate into rings and dip into batter. Drop into 375 degree cooking oil or shortening. When rings are a golden brown drain on a paper towel.

RED NECK PEAS SUPREME

1   cup ham, cooked and diced
1   can of English peas, drained
1   cup of grated mild American cheese
1   can cream of chicken soup
¼   cup diced onion
¼   cup pimento, chopped and drained
1   cup rice, cooked

Mix all ingredients and bake in a greased casserole dish at 325 degrees for 30 minutes.(Optional: may top with French fried onion rings or buttered bread crumbs).

STUFFED ONION POTATOES

4   *large baking potatoes*
2   *large onions, chopped fine*
1   *cup of chopped green onions*
½   *cup chopped mushrooms*
½   *cup cheddar cheese, shredded*
¼   *stick of melted butter*

Core out potatoes leaving skin unharmed. Take inner potatoes and chop for boiling, then boil potatoes till soft and ready for whipping. While waiting for potatoes to boil, bake at 300 degrees; trying not to harm the skins. Whip potatoes as you would mash potatoes. Mix onions and mushrooms into whipped potatoes, adding melted butter and salt and pepper as desired. Then stuff baked potato skins with your whipped potatoes and bake for 20 minutes at 350 degrees. And 5 minutes before removing from oven, sprinkle cheese and green onions on top.

ROZE'S SNOWY POTATOES

4	lbs. Potatoes, peeled and cut up
1	8oz. pack of cream cheese(softened)
1	cup sour cream
2	teaspoon salt
1/8	teaspoon black pepper
1	teaspoon garlic salt
¼	cup chopped chives
½	teaspoon paprika
1	Tablespoon butter or margarine

Cook potatoes in salted water until tender. Drain and mash potatoes in large bowl with electric mixer. Add cream cheese, sour cream, pepper and garlic salt. Beat at high speed until smooth and light. Stir in chives, and spoon into a lightly buttered 10 cup baking dish. Sprinkle with paprika and dot with butter or margarine. Bake at 350 degrees for 30 minutes.

(Note): You may add 1 cup of cheddar cheese to top and bake a few more minutes until cheese is melted.

BILL'S POTATO SALAD

3	cups peeled, boiled, cubed and chilled new potatoes
2	Tablespoons of finely chopped onion
2	hard boiled eggs, finely chopped
½	teaspoon salt
	dash pepper
2/3	cup dairy sour cream
1/3	cup dill or sweet pickle relish
2 ½	Tablespoons of mayonnaise
2	Tablespoons of cider vinegar
1	teaspoon prepared mustard
½	teaspoon celery seed
½	cup chopped green olives(Optional)

In a large bowl, combine potatoes, ½ of eggs, onion, salt and pepper. In a small bowl, combine sour cream, pickle relish, mayonnaise, vinegar, mustard, celery seed and olives. Pour over potato mixture, toss lightly and refrigerate. Before serving garnish with remaining eggs.

IRISH POTATO CASSEROLE

8 to 10 medium potatoes, peeled
1   8oz. package cream cheese, softened
1   8oz. carton commercial sour cream
½   cup butter or margarine, melted
1   clove garlic, minced
*   Paprika*
2   teaspoons salt
¼   cup chopped chives

Cook potatoes in boiling water about 30 minutes or until tender.
Drain potatoes and mash.
Beat cream cheese with an electric mixer until smooth. Add potatoes
and remaining ingredients except paprika; beat just until combined.
Spoon mixture into a lightly buttered 2-quart casserole; sprinkle
with paprika. Cover and refrigerate overnight.
Remove from refrigerator 15 minutes before baking. Uncover and
bake at 350 degrees for 30 minutes or until thoroughly heated.

Yield: 8 to 10 servings

SWEET POTATO SOUFFLE

3	cups sweet potatoes, mashed
1	cup sugar
3	eggs
½	stick of butter or oleo
½	teaspoon salt
1	Tablespoon vanilla
½	cup milk

Combine all ingredients. Pour into baking dish . And top with topping below.

TOPPING:

1	cup brown sugar
½	cup self-rising flour
½	stick butter or oleo
1	cup chopped pecans

Mix and blend by hand all ingredients. Spread on potato mixture. Bake until topping is light brown in a 350 degree oven.

SWEET POTATO CASSEROLE

2	cups sweet potatoes, cooked & mashed
1	cup sugar
½	cup butter
2	eggs, beaten
1	teaspoon vanilla
1/3	cup milk

Mix all ingredients together. Place in baking dish.

TOPPING:

1	cup brown sugar
½	cup self rising flour
1/3	cup butter
1	cup chopped nuts

Mix well, spread on top of casserole. Bake at 350 degrees for 25 minutes.

AUNT ALMA'S RICE CASSEROLE

1	*stick of margarine*
1	*medium onion, chopped*
1 ¼	*cups long grain rice*
1	*can beef consomme*
1	*teaspoon salt*

Saute onions in margarine until transparent. Then combine onions with the other ingredients in a casserole dish. Bake uncovered, in oven at 350 degrees for 1 hour.

WILD RICE CASSEROLE

1   *box wild rice*
1   *medium onion, chopped*
1   *3oz. can sliced mushroom*
½   *bell pepper, chopped*
½   *pound sausage*
      dash of tabasco
1   *teaspoon of Accent*
      salt and pepper
1   *can of cream of mushroom soup*

Prepare rice as instructed on box. Brown sausage in skillet, then saute onions and green pepper. Add crumbled sausage and vegetables to cooked, drained rice. Stir in seasonings and mushroom soup and bake uncovered in a casserole dish for 25 to 30 minutes, at 350 degrees.

GRILLED SQUASH AND ONIONS

6   *medium squash, cut into ½ inch slices*
4   *medium onions, cut into ½ inch slices*
¼   *teaspoon garlic salt*
2   *Tablespoons butter*
    Salt and pepper to taste

Alternate squash and onion slices in rows on large sheet of foil. Sprinkle with garlic salt, salt, pepper and dot with butter. Wrap foil securely to seal. Place on grill over moderate heat for about 45 minutes or until tender.

Yield: 5 to 6 servings.

SQUASH CASSEROLE

2	cups squash, cooked and drained
1	medium onion, chopped
½	stick margarine, melted
1	can cream of chicken soup, undiluted
1	4oz. sour cream
1	egg
2	cups cheese, grated
1	large can French fried onion rings

Mix first seven ingredients together and place in greased casserole dish. Bake at 350 degrees for 30 minutes or until done. Remove from oven and top with French fried onion rings. Brown and serve while hot.

ZUCCHINI CASSEROLE

2   *squash*
3   *Tablespoons sugar*
4   *Tablespoons flour*
1   *medium onion*
1   *pint tomatoes*
1   *green pepper (optional)*
1   *teaspoon salt*
½   *teaspoon oreganos*

TOP WITH

2   *Tablespoons of butter*
1   *cup bread crumbs*
      4oz. sharp cheese

Dice or slice squash. Cook in boiling water 5 minutes. Dice onions and pepper. Brown onion and pepper in butter. Stir in flour and add tomatoes. Stir over low heat until thickened. Add salt and sugar. Layer drained squash into buttered 2 quart casserole. Pour on tomato mixture. Top with grated cheese, bread crumbs, and dot with butter. Bake at 350 degrees for about 45 minutes or until golden brown.

SEAFOOD
CHICKEN
MEAT
AND
GAME

BIG CATCH CASSEROLE

1	package noodles, cooked and drained
½	cup salad dressing
¼	cup milk
¼	cup cheese, shredded
2	eggs, hard boiled & chopped
1	can English peas
1	can salmon, flaked
1	Tablespoon onion, chopped
1	can condensed cream of celery soup
	Paprika

Spread noodles in bottom of casserole dish. Add peas and salmon. Combine salad dressing, onion, milk and soup; pour over salmon. Top with cheese and eggs. Sprinkle with paprika. Bake for 20 minutes at 325 degrees.

Yield: 6 servings

AVA'S CATFISH STEW

2	lbs. fresh catfish nuggets
1	large onion, chopped
1	large green bell pepper, chopped
1	15oz. can of garden peas
½	stick butter
2	cups of milk
1	lb. of salad shrimp
2	medium potatoes, diced

Boil catfish nuggets, covered with water for about 30 minutes or until they become flaky. When done set off burner and keep stock water. Cook onion, pepper and potatoes in 1 ½ cups of water; add more if needed and cook for about 20 minutes. Season to taste with salt and pepper. Combine catfish, shrimp, onion, pepper, potatoes and garden peas and add ½ stick of butter cut into pieces. Boil for 10 to 15 minutes. Set aside and add 2 cups of milk and cook on low heat for 10 minutes(don't boil). Ready for serving.

I like several dashes of hot sauce and oyster crackers. (GREAT)

POP'S CRAB MEAT CASSEROLE

3   cups fresh or canned crab meat
2   Tablespoons chopped chives
1   Tablespoon chopped parsley
½   cup finely chopped celery
1   teaspoon white vinegar
3   Tablespoons butter
       dash of Worcestershire sauce
4   Tablespoons flour
1 ¼   cups milk
1   egg, beaten
       salt and pepper to taste
2   hard boiled eggs, sliced
½   cup grated sharp cheese

Place crab meat in a bowl and remove all particles of shell. Add
chives, parsley, celery, vinegar, and Worcestershire sauce. Melt
butter and stir in flour; add milk and cook (stirring constantly)
until mixture simmers and thickens. Remove from heat and slowly
stir in beaten egg. Add to crab mixture with salt and pepper to taste.
Mix thoroughly. Place half the crab mixture in a greased baking
dish. Cover with a layer of sliced hard boiled eggs. Add remaining
crab mixture and top with cheese. Bake at 350 degrees for about
35 minutes.

SLICK'S CRAB CASSEROLE

1	12oz.can of crab meat
1	cup mayonnaise
1	teaspoon McCormicks seafood seasoning
1	cup canned milk
1	cup bread crumbs
2	Tablespoons butter
1	cup grated cheese

Mix crab meat, milk, mayonnaise and seafood seasoning together and put in 1-quart baking dish. Sprinkle with bread crumbs and dot with butter. Bake at 275 degrees for 45 minutes. Grated cheese can be added as a topping approximately 10 minutes before it is ready to come from the oven.

Yield: 6 servings

CRAB MEAT BISCUIT PIE

1	10 oz. package of frozen mixed vegetables
1	10 ½oz. can cream of mushroom soup
½	cup milk
1	teaspoon of lemon juice
1	16 oz. can of crabmeat
6	refrigerator biscuits
1	cup of grated cheese

Cook and drain mixed vegetables. Preheat oven to 450 degrees. Blend soup, milk and lemon juice in a small bowl and pour into an 8-inch square baking dish. Stir in crabmeat and mixed vegetables; bake for 10 minutes. Stir the baked mixture. Top with a border of biscuits, cut in half. Brush biscuits with butter. Sprinkle with cheese. Bake 8-10 minutes more until biscuits are nicely brown.

BRAD'S SALMON CROQUETTES

1	lb. diced fresh salmon poached in water, lemon juice and white wine
1	medium sweet onion chopped fine
½	stick melted butter
½	cup crushed saltine crackers
1	egg
2	Tablespoons milk
3	Tablespoons self rising flour (plus some for coating)
2	fresh lemons, juiced
3	Tablespoons fresh chopped dill weed
½	cup vegetable oil
1	Tablespoon fresh chopped garlic
1	teaspoon salt
1	Tablespoon pepper

Pour vegetable oil in skillet and set to the side. Then in a large bowl mix all other ingredients including poached salmon. Form mixture into palm size patties, place on tray and let cool in refrigerator for 1 hour. Then heat oil in skillet to med-low. Roll patties in coating and fry to golden brown on both sides.

Yield: 2 to 4 servings.

FRIED OYSTERS

2	eggs
1	pint select oysters
2	cups flour
¼	cup milk
	salt and pepper to taste

Beat eggs and milk together. Salt and pepper oysters. Dip oysters in eggs and milk; then dip in flour and fry until golden brown.

TOOTSIE'S SEAFOOD CHOWDER

1   *large onion, chopped*
1   *bunch of green onions, chopped*
½   *stick of butter*
1   *8 oz. cream cheese*
2   *6 ½ cans of small shrimp*
2   *cans of minced clams*
3   *catfish fillets (microwaved or broiled) cooked and flaked*
3   *10 ½ cans of cream of potato soup*
4   *cups of milk*
    salt and pepper to taste

Saute onions in butter; and add cream cheese and soften. Add Remaining ingredients and simmer for 15 minutes. Stir often. Do not boil. Add more milk before serving.

SHRIMP CASSEROLE

2	lbs. fresh shrimp (boiled & peeled)
1	lb. fresh mushrooms, chopped
1	can cream of chicken soup
1	can of french fried onion rings
2	cups of grated cheese
1	medium onion, chopped

Mix all ingredients except onion rings; put in casserole dish and bake for 30 minutes at 350 degrees. Take out of oven and add the onion rings, placing back in oven until onion rings brown. Serve hot.

CHICKEN CASSEROLE

4	cups chicken, diced, cooked and deboned
1	can cream of chicken soup
1	cup onions, chopped
½	cup bell pepper, chopped
½	cup pimento, diced
1 ½	cup rice, cooked
½	stick margarine, melted
½	cup mayonnaise
1	teaspoon salt
½	teaspoon black pepper
1	small can water chestnuts, sliced and drained
1	small can mushrooms, sliced and drained

Mix all ingredients except crust and place in greased casserole dish . Bake at 350 degrees for 30-35 minutes. Take from oven and top with cracker crumbs and margarine. Return to oven and bake until brown (3 to 5 minutes).

CHICKEN ENCHILADAS

3   *boneless, skinless chicken breast*
1   *large jar of Pace picante sauce*
1   *package of flour tortillas*
1   *8oz. package cream cheese*
½   *cup chopped onions*
2   *cups shredded Mexican cheese or cheddar*

Cut chicken into 11/2 inch pieces and season. Cook in pan over medium heat with a little oil for 5 minutes or until chicken is no longer pink. Remove chicken and set aside. Add onions and saute on low heat(reserve enough picante sauce to top enchiladas). Add picante sauce and cream cheese stirring frequently and then add chicken. Let cool slightly, and grease bottom of pan or glass dish. Spoon a little mixture onto flour tortilla a gently roll. Place in pan; seam side down. Repeat. And pour reserved picante sauce over enchiladas and add cheese. Bake at 350 degrees for 10 to 15 minutes or until cheese is melted.

LINDA'S CHICKEN OR TURKEY CASSEROLE

2	*cups of chicken or turkey, diced*
1	*small container of sour cream*
1	*can cream of celery soup*
1	*can cream of mushroom soup*
1	*can water*
1	*box of Stove Top Stuffing (follow directions on box)*

Dice chicken or turkey and lay in a lightly greased baking dish. In a bowl put small container of sour cream, cream of celery and cream of mushroom soup and a can of water. Mix well. Pour mixture over meat (do not stir). Make Stove Top Stuffing and spoon stuffing over the sour cream and soup mixture(do not stir). Bake for 30 to 45 minutes at 350 degrees or until the top of your stuffing turns brown.

Even better the next day. Serve warm.

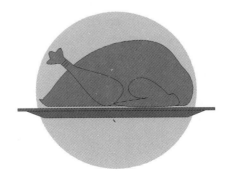

ROAST PRIME RIB
OF BEEF

2   *Tablespoons dark soy sauce*
1 ½   *Tablespoons Kitchen Bouquet*
1   *Tablespoon dry Colman's mustard*
1   *8 to 9 pound beef rib roast, bone in*
1 ½   *cup peeled and (sliced thin) yellow onion*
        Ground black pepper to taste

Rub the seasonings on the roast in the order listed. Pack the sliced onion on the roast. Place the roast on a rack in a roasting pan. Roast in preheated 450 degree oven for 20 minutes. Reduce the oven temperature to 325 degrees and roast 1 hour. Reduce the oven again to 300 degrees and roast about 1 more hour, or until the beef registers 115 degrees for rare in the center when tested with a meat thermometer. Remove from the oven and allow to stand 15 minutes in a warm place. Slice and serve immediately with your favorite sauce for beef.

POLYNESIAN BEEF

1 ½	teaspoons garlic salt
1	teaspoon paprika
1	teaspoon ground ginger
2 ½	lbs. Sirloin steak (cut in 1 ½-inch cubes)
1	large garlic clove, minced
	cooking oil
1	13 oz. can pineapple chunks, drained (reserve syrup)
1	10 ½ oz. can condensed beef broth
¼	cup of garlic flavored wine vinegar
½	cup celery, thinly cut
2	medium onions, sliced
3	large tomatoes, sliced
4	Tablespoons brown sugar
2	Tablespoons corn starch
¼	cup water
3	Tablespoons all purpose soy sauce
½	cup green bell peppers, sliced

Mix garlic salt, paprika and ground ginger thoroughly and toss mixture with meat cubes to coat. Brown meat and garlic in hot skillet using a small amount of cooking oil. Stir in the reserved pineapple syrup, beef broth and ½ of the vinegar. Cover skillet. Simmer gently about 2 hours and stir in celery, onions, tomatoes and pineapple chunks. Cook covered about 10 minutes. Stir in a mixture of brown sugar, corn starch, water, soy sauce and remaining vinegar. Add green bell peppers and bring to boil; stirring gently. Cook 3 minutes. Serve with hot cooked seasoned rice.

SPORTS STEW

2	lbs. of ground beef
2	14.5 oz. cans of diced tomatoes
1	16 oz. box of macaroni twists
1	jumbo onion, chopped
½	stick of butter
	dash of garlic
1	bay leaf
	salt and pepper to taste

If there is something else you like, ADD it.

In a large frying pan; brown ground beef very good, chop up very fine. And set aside. In a very large pot cook a pound of macaroni according to directions on the box. About ¾ of the way through cooking the macaroni, add ground beef, tomatoes, onion, garlic, butter, and bay leaf and more hot water if needed. I like a lot of juice. Keep a close check on it. When done I like several dashes of hot sauce. Serve with your favorite crackers.

PLEASE NOTE: When you think it is done let it sit covered for 1 hour, checking often to be sure you have enough juice. Salt and pepper to taste.

NO PEEK BEEF CASSEROLE

2   *lbs. Stew beef, cut into 1-inch pieces*
1   *envelope of dry onion soup mix*
1   *10 ½oz. can cream of mushroom soup*
1   *4oz. can whole mushrooms*
½   *cup red wine; add water if needed*

Combine all ingredients in crock pot. Stir together well. Cover and cook on low for 8 to 10 hours. Serve over noodles or rice.

CALIFORNIA CHILI

1 ½	cups of dry pinto beans
4	cups water
2	bacon slices, diced
1	garlic clove, crushed
½	teaspoon ground cumin
1	15oz. can of tomato sauce
1	teaspoon salt
1	lb. beef stew meat
1	cup onion, chopped
2	Tablespoons chili powder
5	drops hot pepper sauce

Combine beans and water in a large saucepan. Heat to boiling; boil 2 minutes. Remove from heat and allow to stand covered for 1 hour. Heat to boiling again and reduce heat and boil gently until beans are tender about 1 ½ hours. Add salt to beans for last 30 minutes of cooking. Cut stew meat into 1-inch cubes. Combine bacon and stew meat in large skillet and cook until meat is well browned on all sides. Add onion and garlic to skillet and cook until onion is tender. Stir in tomato sauce, chili powder, cumin, and hot pepper sauce. Cover and boil gently for 1 hour and 15 minutes and add beans. Boil gently covered for 20 to 30 minutes. Stir occasionally.

POT LUCK

3	cups of leftover roast beef or steak cut in ¾ inch cubes
3	Tablespoons bacon fat
1	garlic clove, mashed
1	large onion, sliced
¼	pound mushrooms, sliced
3	Tablespoons flour
2 ½	cups consomme
½	cup red wine
	Salt and pepper to taste
1	teaspoon minced parsley
½	teaspoon marjoram
1	teaspoon Worcestershire sauce
	Pastry or biscuit for crust

This is one of the most appetizing dishes that can be made of leftover roast beef or steak, a problem that faces most cooks at one time or another.

Melt fat in heavy skillet and saute garlic, onion and mushrooms until onion begins to take on color. Stir in meat and saute lightly a few minutes. Sprinkle flour over and mix well. Pour on consomme and wine, stirring constantly until sauce is smooth and thickened. Season to taste and add herbs and Worcestershire sauce. Pour in 2-quart casserole and top with either rolled pastry, slashed to allow steam to escape, or small baking powder biscuits. Bake in hot oven, 450 degrees about 20 minutes, or until top is golden brown.

SPAGHETTI SAUCE WITH MEATBALLS

Meatballs:

1	lb. hamburger meat
	salt and pepper to taste
1	Tablespoon ground parsley
¼	cup bread crumbs
¼	teaspoon garlic powder
½	teaspoon grated garlic
1	egg

Mix these ingredients together and form into meat balls; the size you prefer. Fry slowly in oil. Do not brown, they'll finish cooking in the sauce.

Sauce:

1	lb. pork sausage (mild or Italian seasoned)
2	cans Italian tomato paste (not sauce or puree)
1	medium can tomatoes
	salt and pepper to taste
1	can mushroom slices
2	cans mushroom sauce
	(If you can't find it in a store, it can be made by running mushroom stems and pieces through a blender with enough liquid to make a sauce like in consistency).
3	sections garlic, diced fine
1	teaspoon garlic powder

Fry pork sausage slowly, while breaking it up with fork(don't brown). After it is done, add remainder of ingredients and mix well. Add meat balls; cover and cook slowly for 3 to 4 hours. Stir occasionally.

If sauce is too thin, sprinkle with grated Parmesan cheese or other Italian cheese. If too thick add water.

EASY MEAT LOAF

2	lb. hamburger
2	onions, finely chopped
1	teaspoon salt
1	teaspoon pepper
10	slices bread
2	eggs
3	stalks celery, finely chopped
1	can tomato soup
1	small bell pepper, chopped

Combine all ingredients; shape into loaf. Place in baking pan. Cover with ketchup. Bake at 325 degrees for 1 hour.

Yield: 8 servings.

MEXICAN SALAD

1   *lb. ground beef*
¼   *cup chopped onion*
1   *16oz. can kidney beans, drained*
½   *cup French dressing*
½   *cup of water*
2   *Tablespoon of chili powder*
3   *cups of shredded lettuce*
½   *cup of green onion slices*
2   *cups shredded sharp cheddar cheese*

Brown meat and drain. Add onion; and cook until tender. Stir in beans, dressing, water and chili powder. Simmer 15 minutes. Combine lettuce and green onion and add meat mixture and 11/2 cups cheese; mix lightly. Top with remaining cheese

Yield: 4 to 6 servings

STUFFED PEPPERS

1 ½	lbs. ground beef
1	can tomato sauce
2	eggs, beaten
½	teaspoon pepper
1	large onion, chopped
2	cups cooked rice
3	teaspoons salt
12	medium green peppers

Mix first 7 ingredients well; set aside. Cut out pepper centers; remove seeds and stems. Wash well; drain. Stuff peppers with meat mixture and place on baking sheet. Bake at 350 degrees for 45 to 60 minutes or until meat is done. May be baked and frozen for later use.

BEEF AND CORN CHEESE BAKE

1	*lb. ground beef*
⅓	*cup onion, chopped*
1	*can Campbell's cheddar cheese soup*
⅓	*cup water*
2	*cups cooked noodles*
1	*cup tomatoes, drained and chopped*
1	*teaspoon prepared mustard*
1	*8oz. can whole kernel golden corn, drained*

In a skillet, brown beef and cook onion until tender. Use shortening if necessary. Stir to separate meat; pour off fat. Stir in remaining ingredients. Pour into 1 1/2-quart casserole dish. Bake at 350 degrees for 35 minutes or until hot. Stir and garnish with parsley.

GROUND BEEF AND CABBAGE SUPREME

1 ½   teaspoon salt
1   lb. ground beef
1   small head of cabbage, chopped
1   teaspoon pepper
1   large onion, chopped
½   cup water

Mix ½ teaspoon of salt and ½ teaspoon pepper, ground beef, and onion; place in skillet and cook until slightly browned. Add cabbage, and remaining salt and pepper and water. Cover and simmer for 30 minutes or until cabbage is tender and liquid has evaporated.

CHEESEBURGER PIE

1	lb. hamburger, browned and drained
½	cup chopped onion, sauteed
3	eggs
1 ½	cups milk
	salt and pepper to taste
2	cups grated cheddar cheese
¾	cup Bisquick

Place hamburger and onion in greased 10 inch pie plate. Cover with cheese and salt and pepper to taste. Blend milk and eggs and Bisquick in blender for 30 seconds and pour over meat and cheese mixture. Bake for 30 minutes at 350 degrees.

BERNIE'S ONIONS WITH LIVER

1 ½	lbs. calves or baby beef liver, cut in 1 inch strips
½	teaspoon salt
1/8	teaspoon pepper
¼	cup of butter or bacon drippings
2	onions, thinly sliced
1	8oz. can sliced mushrooms, undrained
2	cups dairy sour cream
1	teaspoon Worcestershire sauce

Season liver with salt and pepper. Preheat skillet to 325 degrees. Melt butter and saute onions until tender. Add liver and brown on all sides. Add mushrooms with liquid; reduce heat to simmer. Simmer covered with vent closed for 8-10 minutes. Add sour cream and continue cooking for and additional 8-10 minutes. Add Worcestershire sauce.

NOT RUN OF THE MILL PORK CHOPS

2   *Tablespoons shortening*
8   *loin chops, ¾-inch thick*
1   *medium onion, sliced 1/8-inch thick*
1   *4oz. can of sliced mushrooms, drained*
½   *cup water chestnuts*
¼   *cup soy sauce*
¼   *cup water*
2   *Tablespoons lemon juice*
½   *teaspoon ground ginger*
¼   *teaspoon garlic powder*

Heat shortening in skillet on medium heat. When grease gets hot enough add chops and brown well on both sides. Pour off any fat. Arrange onion slices, mushrooms and water chestnuts on chops. Combine remaining ingredients and pour over chops. Cover and bake in 350 degree oven for 45 minutes or until chops are tender.

Yield: 6 to 8 servings.

HOBO'S DREAM

3   *Tablespoons cooking oil*
      6 to 8 pork chops
1   *medium onion, chopped*
      salt and pepper
1   *15oz. can of pork and beans*

Salt and pepper chops to taste. Brown chops and onions in oil. Combine chops and beans in casserole dish. Cover and bake at 350 degrees for 45 minutes.

BACON 'N CHEESE PUFF PIE

10	slices of bacon, cut into 1-inch pieces
1	can of Pillsbury Crescent dinner rolls
2	medium tomatoes, sliced
½	teaspoon salt
	pepper
5	slices of American cheese
3	eggs, separated
¾	cup dairy sour cream
½	cup all purpose flour
	paprika

Fry bacon until crisp; drain. Unroll crescent dough and separate into 8 triangles. Place dough triangles in ungreased 9-inch pie pan, pressing together to form a crust. Sprinkle bacon over crust. Top with tomato slices; season with salt and pepper. Place cheese slices over top. Beat egg whites until stiff. Set aside. In a large mixing bowl, combine egg yolks, sour cream, flour, salt and a dash of pepper. Blend well. Gently fold beaten egg whites into mixture until a few lumps of egg white remain. Do not over blend. Pour mixture over cheese layer. Sprinkle with paprika. Bake at 350 degrees for 35 to 40 minutes or until crust and top are golden brown and knife inserted in center comes out clean.

OLD FASHION FARM FRY

6   slices bacon, diced
4   medium boiled potatoes, diced
2   Tablespoons chopped onion
½   teaspoon salt
¼   teaspoon pepper
1   cup grated sharp cheddar cheese
5   eggs, slightly beaten

In a large skillet over medium heat, fry bacon until crisp. Drain off all but 1 or 2 Tablespoons of fat; add potatoes, onion, salt and pepper. Cook until potatoes are an ivory color. Sprinkle with cheese and add eggs. Stir quickly until eggs are set. Serve at once.

Yield: 4 servings

SAWMILL CHICKEN

10   slices of fresh streak of lean, unsalted
Rinse with hot water; salt and pepper to taste. Roll in self rising
flour and fry in vegetable oil at medium heat until golden
brown. Goes very good with Syrup and Biscuits

ST. PAUL'S RICE & SAUSAGE CASSEROLE

1	lb. hot or mild sausage, mashed up fine
2	4.2 oz. packages of Lipton Noodles & Sauce, Creamy Chicken
1	cup raw rice
1	large green bell pepper, chopped
1	large onion, chopped
1	stalk celery, chopped
5 ½	cups water
½	cup Almonds, sliced

Brown 1 lb. of hot or mild sausage and mash up fine; set aside. Chop one large green bell pepper, one large onion, and one stalk of celery. In a large pot add 2 packages of Lipton Noodles & Sauce and 1 cup of raw rice and then add 5 ½ cups of water and boil for 7 minutes. Mix all ingredients together and pour into a 9.5x13.5x2 inch (3 quart) baking dish; and sprinkle with ½ cup of sliced Almonds. Bake at 350 degrees for 1 hour.

CANADIAN GOOSE BREAST

2   *large goose breast*
6   *large bay leaves*
1   *26oz. can cream of mushroom soup*
½   *cup green onions, chopped*
½   *teaspoon salt*
½   *teaspoon coarse ground pepper*

Place bay leaves on bottom of slow cooker; place goose breast on top of bay leaves. Top with soup, green onions, salt and pepper. Cook on #2 setting for 10-12 hours, serve over mashed potatoes along with a vegetable. Duck also works well.

TONI'S FRIED QUAIL

4   *quail split in half*
½   *cup of self rising flour*
1   *medium onion*
       salt and pepper to taste

Rinse quail off to make sure it's clean. Heat cooking oil in a deep frying pan and make sure frying pan is ¾ full. Then flour each half of quail and add salt and pepper. Turning occasionally; cook until golden brown and remove from pan.

Gravy:

Pour excess cooking oil out of pan and leave meat drippings. Slice onion into small pieces and saute'. Then add ¼ cup of flour and stir constantly(don't let flour burn) add a glass of hot water and simmer. Stirring constantly.

Serve with rice and hot biscuits.

83

WESTERN ONION BITS BAR-B-Q SAUCE

1   *gallon white vinegar*
1   *gallon ketchup*
1   *large lemon, juiced*
1   *jumbo onion, chopped fine*
¼   *cup pure prepared mustard*
¼   *cup Worcestershire sauce*
1   *teaspoon salt*
2   *teaspoons onion salt*
1   *teaspoon garlic salt*
2   *teaspoon of liquid smoke*
1   *teaspoon paprika*
2   *cups sugar*
3   *teaspoons black pepper*
4   *teaspoons soy sauce*
2   *teaspoons hot sauce*
½   *stick of butter*

Combine all ingredients and bring to a rolling boil. Stirring almost constantly, let boil for 10 to 15 minutes; then simmer for about 2 hours. Simply delicious on all meats.

GRANNY PRICE'S FISH SAUCE

¼   *cup Worcestershire sauce*
2   *Tablespoons vinegar*
¼   *cup sugar*
1   *cup ketchup*
1   *cup grated sweet onions*

Cook 5 minutes on slow heat on top of stove to serve over fish or any seafood.

Recipe Notes

DESSERTS

APPLE DAPPLE CAKE

3	eggs
2	cups sugar
1	teaspoon salt
2	teaspoon vanilla
1 ½	cups chopped nuts (optional)
1 ½	cups salad oil
3	cups all purpose flour
1	teaspoon soda
2	cups apples, chopped

Mix eggs, salad oil and sugar; blend well. Add flour, salt and soda; mix well. Add vanilla, chopped apples and nuts. Pour into a greased 8 or 9 inch tube pan. Bake at 350 degrees for 1 hour.

Hot Topping:

1	cup brown sugar
¼	cup milk (evaporated milk gives good flavor)
1	stick margarine

Combine all ingredients and cook for 1 ½ minutes. Pour over hot cake. Let set until completely cool and then remove from pan.

APPLE DUMPLIN CAKE

1 ½   cup vegetable oil
3   eggs
3   cups self rising flour
1 ½   cups chopped pecans
2   cups sugar
2   teaspoons vanilla
3   cups raw apples, chopped

Combine first 4 ingredients; mix well. Add flour, apples, and pecans. Bake in tube pan at 350 degrees for 1 hour.

Frosting:

1   cup brown sugar
¼   cup milk
½   stick margarine

Combine all ingredients; cook for 3 minutes. Pour over cake while still hot.

COCONUT CAKE

1 cup margarine
2 cups sugar
4 eggs
3 cups self rising flour
1 cup milk
1 teaspoon vanilla

Cream the margarine and sugar. Add eggs one at a time, beating well. Add flour alternating with milk; ending with flour. Add vanilla. Bake at 350 degrees in three 9 or 10 inch pans for 25 to 30 minutes.

Frosting:

2 cups sugar
2/3 cup water
½ teaspoon cream of tartar
4 egg whites
1 teaspoon vanilla
   dash salt
1 16oz. package Angel Flake Coconut

In a sauce pan, combine sugar, water, cream of tartar and salt; bring to boiling. Stirring until sugar dissolves. Boil 2 to 3 minutes. In a large mixer bowl; very slowly add hot syrup to 4 egg whites and vanilla. Beat constantly on high speed about 7 minutes or until stiff peak form. Spread between layers and on top and sides, adding coconut on each layer.

DIRT CAKE

1	small chocolate pound cake, crumbled
1	small white pound cake, crumbled
1	small box chocolate or vanilla instant pudding
1	large cool whip
1	artificial flower
1	bag gummy worms

In a large clear bowl; layer the first 4 ingredients and top with crushed Oreo cookies. Display gummy worms and flower to look like a plant. Chill overnight.

MISSISSIPPI MUD CAKE

2   sticks of butter
2   cups of sugar
½   cup cocoa
1   teaspoon vanilla
1 ½   cup of self rising flour
4   eggs
1 ½   cups chopped pecans
       Miniature marshmallows

Mix ingredients in order given until batter is smooth. Stir in pecans. Pour into a 13x9 inch baking pan and bake 40-45 minutes in a 350 degree oven. While cake is hot, cover with marshmallows and return to oven until marshmallows turn brown and puff up. Top with frosting.

Frosting:

1   stick butter
1   box of powdered sugar
¼   cup cocoa
1   teaspoon vanilla
1/3   cup milk

Sift sugar and cocoa. Cream butter with sugar and cocoa. Add vanilla and milk as needed. Spread over cake and cut into serving pieces.

LONGHAUL OATMEAL CAKE

1	cup oatmeal
1	cup corn oil
2	cup brown sugar
2	cup white sugar
2	eggs
1 ½	cup self-rising flour
¼	teaspoon salt
¼	teaspoon soda
½	teaspoon cinnamon
1	stick margarine
1	teaspoon vanilla
¾	cup milk
1	cup coconut
1	cup chopped nuts

Pour 1 ½ cups boiling water over oatmeal; let stand. Blend oil, 1 cup brown sugar and 1 cup white sugar; beat in eggs. Sift flour, salt, soda and cinnamon together; add to egg mixture. Stir in oatmeal; pour into cake pan. Bake at 350 degrees for 25-30 minutes. Combine remaining ingredients; cook until thickened. Spread on warm cake.

ORANGE CAKE

1	box of yellow cake mix
1	small box of instant vanilla pudding
1	cup of sunny delight
½	cup of oil
½	cup of chopped pecans
4	eggs

Heat oven to 350 degrees and grease and flour the bundt pan; spread nuts evenly on bottom of pan. Combine all other ingredients and pour into pan. Bake of 45 to 50 minutes.

Glaze:

½	cup of butter
½	cup of sugar
½	cup of sunny delight

DOUBLE PEANUT BUTTER
CAKE AND ICING

Cake:

2/3	*cup butter or margarine*
2 ½	*cups sugar*
3 ¾	*cups sifted flour*
2 ¼	*teaspoons baking powder*
1	*Tablespoon vanilla*
2/3	*cup peanut butter*
3	*eggs, beaten*
2 ½	*teaspoons baking soda*
2 ½	*cups buttermilk*

Cream together the butter, peanut butter and sugar. Add beaten eggs to creamed mixture. Sift the flour, baking soda and baking powder together and add alternately with buttermilk and vanilla to creamed mixture. Pour into a greased and lightly floured baking pan 13x9x2 inches. Bake in a preheated 350 degree oven for 35 minutes. Frost with peanut butter icing.

Icing:

1 ½	*cups butter or margarine*
6	*cups confectioners' sugar*
1 ½	*cups pineapple juice*
3	*cups peanut butter*
1 ½	*Tablespoons vanilla*

Cream together the butter and peanut butter. Add powdered sugar, vanilla and enough pineapple juice to make the frosting spread easily.

PEA PICKING CAKE

1	box of yellow butter cake mix
1	8 oz. can of mandarin oranges and juice
½	cup of vegetable oil
2	eggs

Combine ingredients; mix well. Bake at 350 degrees for 25 minutes. Makes 3 layers. Use 3 9-inch baking pans; fill each half full.

Icing:

1	small box of vanilla instant pudding (follow directions on box)
1	16 oz. container of cool whip
2	8 ¼ oz. cans of crushed pineapple, drained

Mix and spread on layers. Put in freezer for 1 hour before serving.

This cake is great for social gatherings or just a good gossip session.

BUTTER POUND CAKE

3	cups cake flour
3	cups sugar
1	lb. Butter
1	small can pet milk
6	eggs
1	Tablespoon vanilla

Blend sugar and butter until creamy; then add one egg at a time and blend. Add 2 cups of flour to mix and stir. Add 1 cup of flour and the can of milk to mix and stir; now add vanilla. Bake at 325 degrees for 1 hour.

SOUR CREAM POUND CAKE

2	*sticks of butter(not margarine)*
3	*cups sugar*
6	*large eggs*
3	*cups of cake flour*
½	*teaspoon baking powder*
¼	*teaspoon salt*
1	*teaspoon vanilla*
1	*cup of sour cream*

Cream butter and sugar, and add eggs one at a time; beating well after each addition. Mix flour with salt and baking powder and add this to the mixture. Fold in sour cream and add vanilla. Grease and flour bundt pan well. Bake at 300 degrees for 2 hours.

BANANA, STRAWBERRY PIE

1   *pt. Frozen strawberries*
½   *cup sugar*
3   *Tablespoons cornstarch*
        Several drops of red food coloring
2   *large bananas*
1   *baked pie shell*

Thaw strawberries; drain juice into measuring cup. Add enough water to make 1 ½ cups liquid. Pour into saucepan; stir in sugar and cornstarch. Cook over low heat until thick and clear, stirring constantly. Stir in food coloring; let stand until cool. Fold in strawberries gently. Slice bananas into pie shell; pour strawberries over bananas. Chill for at least 2 hours before serving. Top with frozen dessert topping, whipped cream or ice cream.

RHUBARB CUSTARD PIE

1   *unbaked pie shell*
2   *cups of cut up rhubarb*
¾   *teaspoon cinnamon*
4   *eggs*
1 ½   *cups of sugar (40 packets of equal if on a sugar free diet)*

Put cut up rhubarb in crust and pour the other 3 ingredients together over rhubarb. Bake at 450 degree for 10 minutes. Then reduce heat to 350 degrees for about an hour or until done.

CINDY'S SINFUL PEACH COBBLER

5	*cups of fresh peaches*
1	*cup of sugar*
1	*cup of sifted self rising flour*
1	*Tablespoon of baking powder*
1	*cup of milk*
1	*stick of butter*

Preheat oven to 350 degrees. In a baking dish mix peaches, sugar, and melted butter. In a separate bowl mix sifted flour and baking powder well. Then slowly add milk to flour to mixture. Stir until all is liquid; then pour over peaches in baking dish. **Do not stir with peaches.** *Place covered baking dish in oven and cook for ½ hour then remove lid. Then finish cooking ½ hour until golden brown.*

Yields: 6 to 10 servings.

SALTED NUT ROLL

1   *box of sour cream cake mix*
2/3   *cups of butter or margarine*
1   *egg*
2   *cups of mini marshmallows*

Combine ingredients into 9 x 13 pan. Bake at 350 for 10-12 minutes. Cover with 2 cups of marshmallows or more if you like. Return to oven until marshmallows begin to ruff (about 2-3 minutes).

1   *12oz. package of peanut butter chips*
2/3   *cup white syrup*
¼   *cups margarine*

Melt all together then add 2 cups salted peanuts. Put on top of warm marshmallows. Cool, cut and cover

Reorder Additional Copies:

Jim Wynn Farms
P.O. Box 730 • Lumber City, GA 31549

Please send me _____ copies of *The Truck Driver's Cookbook* at $19.95 each plus $2.95 each for postage and handling. Each book comes packaged in a most unique burlap bag. Georgia residents please include 7% sales tax.

Name: _____

Address: _____

City: _____ State: _____ Zip: _____

Telephone: _____

- -

Reorder Additional Copies:

Jim Wynn Farms
P.O. Box 730 • Lumber City, GA 31549

Please send me _____ copies of *The Truck Driver's Cookbook* at $19.95 each plus $2.95 each for postage and handling. Each book comes packaged in a most unique burlap bag. Georgia residents please include 7% sales tax.

Name: _____

Address: _____

City: _____ State: _____ Zip: _____

Telephone: _____

- -

Reorder Additional Copies:

Jim Wynn Farms
P.O. Box 730 • Lumber City, GA 31549

Please send me _____ copies of *The Truck Driver's Cookbook* at $19.95 each plus $2.95 each for postage and handling. Each book comes packaged in a most unique burlap bag. Georgia residents please include 7% sales tax.

Name: _____

Address: _____

City: _____ State: _____ Zip: _____

Telephone: _____